Virginia, My State
Biographies

Arthur R. Ashe, Jr.

By Moira Rose Donohue

Clarke C. Scott, M. A.
Content Consultant

Your State • Your Standards • Your Grade Level

Dear Educators, Librarians and Parents . . .

Thank you for choosing this *"Virginia, My State"* series book! We have designed this series to support the Virginia Department of Education's **Standards of Learning for Virginia curriculum studies AND leveled reading**. Each book in the series has been written based on *documented facts at grade level* as measured by the ATOS Readability Formula for Books (Accelerated Reader), the Lexile Framework for Reading, and the Fountas & Pinnell Benchmark Assessment System for Guided Reading. Photographs and/or illustrations, captions and other design elements have been included to provide supportive visual messaging to enhance text comprehension. Glossary and Index sections introduce key new words and help young readers develop skills in locating and combining information. We wish you all success in using this *"Virginia, My State"* series to meet your student or child's learning needs!

Jill Ward, President

Publisher

State Standards Publishing, LLC
1788 Quail Hollow
Hamilton, GA 31811
USA
1.866.740.3056
www.statestandardspublishing.com

Library of Congress Control Number: 2012931647

ISBN-13: 978-1-935884-58-3   hardcover
ISBN-13: 978-1-935884-64-4   paperback

About the Author

Moira Rose Donohue has a Bachelor of Arts in political science from Mississippi University for Women and a Juris Doctorate degree from Santa Clara University School of Law. She was a banking legislative lawyer for 20 years before she began writing for children. Moira is a published author of numerous poems, plays, and articles, as well as two picture books. She loves dogs and tap dancing and lives in northern Virginia with her family.

About the Content Consultant

Clarke C. Scott holds degrees from Central Michigan University and has 31 years of experience as a classroom teacher, building principal and system-wide administrator. Clarke currently serves as Director of Middle School Education and Lead Director for History with Pittsylvania County Schools in Virginia. He enjoys hiking, kayaking, caving, and exploring Virginia's and our nation's history. He shares his adventures both above and underground with his wife, Joyce, and three grown children.

1 2 3 4 5 – CG – 16 15 14 13 12

Table of Contents

Hi, I'm Bagster! Let's learn about important Virginians.

Arthur Ashe was born in Richmond.

Time Line

1943
Born

Home Court

Arthur Robert Ashe, Jr. was born in Richmond, Virginia, on July 10, 1943. Richmond was a **segregated** city at that time, like the rest of the South. Black people and white people went to separate restaurants, churches, and movie theaters. They had separate schools and public spaces. When Arthur was four, his father got a job as a caretaker at a segregated park for blacks. The Ashes moved to a house right in the middle of the playground!

Arthur loved sports and enjoyed living in the park. But he was skinny and sickly. His father wouldn't let him play football. What could Arthur do? The park had swimming pools, baseball fields, and four tennis courts. Arthur learned that being fast and **agile** was important for some of these sports. The tennis courts became very important to Arthur as he grew older.

When Arthur was only six, two things happened that would change his life. First, his mother died suddenly after an operation. Arthur had only a few pictures of her. Second, Arthur met Ron Charity. Ron was a talented African American tennis player.

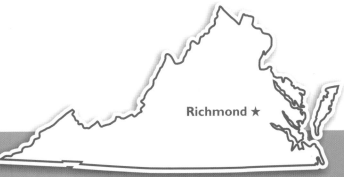

Richmond ★

Shake Hands with the Racket

One day, while Ron Charity was practicing at the playground, he saw Arthur. Ron asked Arthur if he wanted to learn to play tennis. Arthur ran to the equipment box and picked out a tennis racket. Ron taught him to hold the racket with an Eastern grip. "It's like shaking hands," he told Arthur. He taught Arthur how to serve the ball and put it into play. Soon, Arthur was playing tennis.

Ron could tell that Arthur was a gifted tennis player. In 1953, Ron introduced Arthur to Dr. Robert Johnson. "Dr. J" had trained a famous African American tennis player named Althea Gibson. Dr. J agreed to coach Arthur. Arthur knew he was very lucky to be able to work with Dr. J. Sometimes he and Dr. J would take the bus to travel to tennis **matches**. But because they were African Americans, they had to sit in the back of the bus.

 Althea Gibson was the first African American woman to win at the Wimbledon and U.S. Open tennis matches.

Time Line—◯
1943
Born

Arthur learned to shake hands with the racket, like this boy.

Tennis Today

Describe what you see. How is this scene the same or different from tennis today?

Tennis was once played only in private clubs for white people.

Time Line

1943
Born

1960 Moves
to St. Louis

White Person's Game

When tennis was first played in England, it was played by British royalty. In the United States, tennis was once played only in private clubs called country clubs. The clubs did not allow African Americans to join. Arthur Ashe later said, "Some folks call tennis a rich people's sport or a white person's game. I guess I started too early because I just thought it was something fun to do."

Arthur was only twelve when he started playing in tennis **tournaments**. Sometimes he experienced **racism** because he was African American. One time, some white players at a tennis match destroyed property. They blamed Arthur! But other times, Arthur found friendly players. In Charlottesville, Arthur went to the movies with a group of white tennis players. The ticket seller wouldn't sell Arthur a ticket, so all the boys refused to go in!

Arthur wanted to practice all the time, even in the winter. But there were no indoor courts for African Americans in Richmond. So in 1960, Arthur moved to St. Louis, Missouri. His father had to stay behind with Arthur's younger brother. Arthur lived with some of Dr. J's friends while in St. Louis.

The Way You Play

Arthur was a senior in high school when he moved to St. Louis. He graduated at the top of his class. Then he got an athletic **scholarship** to the University of California at Los Angeles, called UCLA. Arthur had played a lot of tennis matches by then. At UCLA, Arthur was captain of the tennis team. He led the team to win a national college championship, the NCAA championship.

Arthur's father always told him it was important to be a good person. Arthur's coach, Dr. J, taught him to lose with a smile and stay calm. Arthur listened. He was already becoming known for his controlled behavior on the

tennis court. "I've heard . . . you can tell someone's personality by the way they play tennis," Arthur once said.

In 1963, Arthur made the Davis Cup tennis team for the United States. It was the first time an African American was on the team. Arthur was becoming famous.

Time Line

1943 Born

1960 Moves to St. Louis

1963 Makes Davis Cup team

Arthur was becoming known for his controlled behavior on the tennis court.

Arthur went to the United States Military Academy at West Point.

Time Line

| 1943 Born | 1960 Moves to St. Louis | 1963 Makes Davis Cup team |

A Different Kind of "Serve"

Arthur studied hard at UCLA. He went to Australia with the Davis Cup team in 1965. But that meant he had to put off graduation for a year. He also had to make a decision about serving in the Army. The United States was fighting a war in Vietnam. Arthur decided to join the Reserve Officers' Training Corps, called ROTC. This way, he could be trained as an officer in the military. In 1966, Arthur earned his college degree in business. Then the Army sent him to the United States Military Academy at West Point, New York. Arthur was now in the Army.

While Arthur was at West Point, he became more aware of the **civil rights movement**. People were working for equal rights for African Americans. In 1968, a friend of Dr. Martin Luther King, Jr. asked Arthur to make a speech. Dr. King was a leader in the civil rights movement. Arthur agreed to make the speech. But his speech was not against white people. Instead, he said that African Americans should show the world that they were as good as whites. The *Washington Post* newspaper's headline wrote, "Ashe Becomes Activist." An **activist** is a person who speaks out about a problem or a political cause. But the Army told Arthur not to make any more political speeches. It was against Army rules.

"Well Done, Son"

While serving at West Point, Arthur still played tennis. In the summer of 1968, he played in the U. S. Open tennis tournament. It was his first *Grand Slam* tournament. It was one of the most important tournaments in tennis. In the final match, Arthur played against Tom Okker, a professional player from the Netherlands. Professional players earn a living playing tennis. They can accept money to play. Arthur was only an amateur player. Amateurs play for fun and cannot accept money to play. But Arthur played so well that he won the tournament! It was the first time an African American man had won the U. S. Open! Arthur stood with his father at the final awards ceremony. His father had tears in his eyes. He whispered to Arthur, "Well done, son."

Arthur went on to win his second *Grand Slam* tournament in 1970. It was called the Australian Open.

 There are four *Grand Slam* tennis tournaments: the U. S. Open, the Australian Open, the French Open, and Wimbledon. A player wins the *Grand Slam* by winning all four tournaments in one year.

Time Line

| 1943 Born | 1960 Moves to St. Louis | 1963 Makes Davis Cup team | 1968 Wins U.S. Open |

Arthur's father said, "Well done, son."

Arthur became the first African American man to win at Wimbledon.

Time Line

| 1943 Born | 1960 Moves to St. Louis | 1963 Makes Davis Cup team | 1968 Wins U.S. Open | 1975 Wins at Wimbledon |

Match Point

Arthur became a professional tennis player. He began playing in matches all over the world. One year, he played on five continents. He especially wanted to play tennis in South Africa. At that time, South Africa had a system of government called **apartheid**. Under apartheid, people were treated differently according to their race. Arthur wanted to learn about life in South Africa. He hoped to serve as a role model to black South Africans. But to visit, he had to get official permission, called a **visa**. He applied for one in 1969 but he didn't get it. Arthur was not allowed to visit South Africa. He could not play tennis there because he was black! Finally in 1973, Arthur got his visa. When he saw the effects of apartheid in South Africa, he became very upset. He would work for many years to try to end apartheid.

Arthur still had more tennis to play. In 1975, Arthur traveled to England to play at Wimbledon. Jimmy Connors, the number-one player in the world, was the favorite to win. But Arthur shocked the world. He won the match and became the first African American man to win at Wimbledon.

Africa

South Africa

A Life-Changing Picture

During the next year, Arthur won five more tennis tournaments. He also met Jeanne Moutoussamy. She was a photographer and wanted to take his picture. Arthur and Jeanne fell in love and were married in 1977. The wedding took place at the United Nations in New York City. Years later, Arthur and Jeanne had a daughter. They wanted her to have a very special name. Can you guess what it was? They called her Camera.

In July 1979, Arthur was teaching tennis to disadvantaged children in New York when he had a heart attack. Six months later, Arthur had to have heart surgery. Sadly, he soon realized that his days of playing in tennis tournaments were over. Arthur retired from competition in 1980 with 818 wins, 260 losses, and 51 titles.

 Arthur was born in July, 1943—he had a heart attack in July, 1979. Do the math—he was only 36 years old!

Time Line

1943 Born   **1960** Moves to St. Louis   **1963** Makes Davis Cup team   **1968** Wins U.S. Open   **1975** Wins at Wimbledon

Arthur married a photographer named Jeanne Moutoussamy.

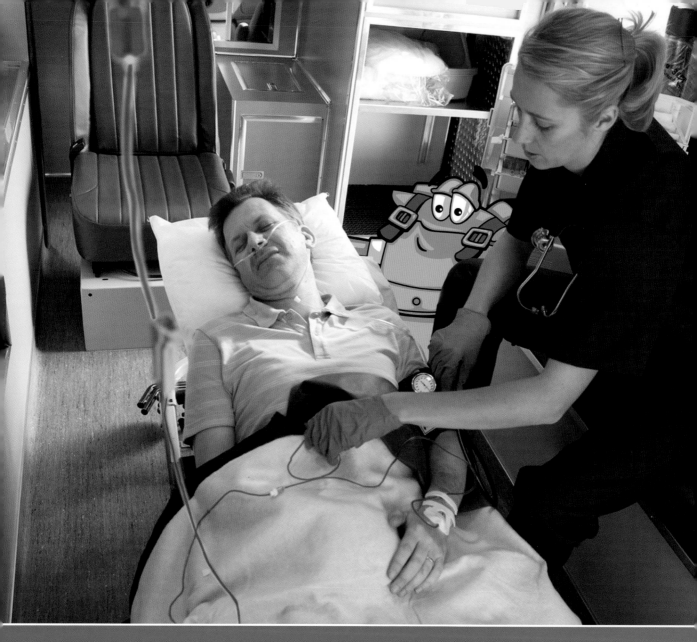

Arthur had to have a blood transfusion, like this man.

Time Line

1943 Born	**1960** Moves to St. Louis	**1963** Makes Davis Cup team	**1968** Wins U.S. Open	**1975** Wins at Wimbledon

Honors and Illness

Even though Arthur couldn't compete, he stayed involved in tennis. In 1980, he was asked to be the captain of the Davis Cup team. It was a great honor. He was captain for five years. The team won in 1981 and 1982. As captain, Arthur had to coach John McEnroe. McEnroe was the opposite of Arthur. Arthur was always calm while McEnroe was often angry and yelled a lot. But they got along.

During this time, Arthur also wrote books about tennis. But his health became a problem for him again. In 1983, Arthur needed another operation on his heart. Because he was weak after the surgery, doctors gave him a blood **transfusion**. But Arthur got better again.

In 1985, Arthur got some good news. He had been voted into the International Tennis Hall of Fame. He went with his family to the ceremony in Newport, Rhode Island. Arthur called it the "honor of a lifetime."

Davis Cup

More Bad News

Remember Arthur's visit to South Africa? He had seen many whites-only signs that reminded him of Richmond when it was segregated. In 1985, he decided to take part in a protest in Washington, D. C. against apartheid. He knew he would probably be arrested for protesting, and he was! Being arrested was very hard for Arthur because he had always been a model of good behavior. But he felt so strongly about South Africa that he knew he had to speak out.

Three years later, Arthur found that he had no feeling in his hand. The doctors examined him and decided he needed brain surgery. But the news was even worse than that. The doctors learned that Arthur had a virus called HIV. They believed the blood Arthur received during the transfusion in 1983 was **contaminated** with the virus.

Under apartheid in South Africa, blacks did not have the same rights as whites, including the right to vote in national elections. They were not allowed in the same places. Fortunately, South Africa began to end apartheid in 1990. By 1994, everyone in South Africa had the right to vote in elections. Many people, like Arthur, helped bring about this positive change.

Time Line

| 1943 Born | 1960 Moves to St. Louis | 1963 Makes Davis Cup team | 1968 Wins U.S. Open | 1975 Wins at Wimbledon |

Arthur saw many whites-only signs in South Africa, like this one.

At the United Nations, Arthur told the world about his terrible disease.

Time Line

| 1943 Born | 1960 Moves to St. Louis | 1963 Makes Davis Cup team | 1968 Wins U.S. Open | 1975 Wins at Wimbledon |

What We Give

The HIV virus in Arthur's body turned into a disease called AIDS. It is a very serious disease. Arthur was often very sick. He knew that there was no cure. But Arthur had always been **optimistic**. He was a positive thinker. On his good days, Arthur still worked to help with tennis programs for disadvantaged children. He still worked to support equal treatment for all races. Arthur once said, "From what we get, we can make a living; what we give, however, makes a life."

In 1992, Arthur announced to the public that he had AIDS. It was hard to tell the world about his terrible disease. It was also hard to tell his young daughter, Camera. In December of that year, he gave a speech to the United Nations. He thought it was one of the most important speeches of his life. He spoke about his disease. And he encouraged people to raise money to help find a cure for AIDS.

Every Christmas, Arthur took Camera to visit poor families. They gave away toys, including some of Camera's own new ones.

1977
Marries

1985 Enters
Tennis Hall of Fame

1992
Addresses U. N.

25

A First at the Last

Arthur made plans for a Valentine's Day dance in 1993. But AIDS had made his body weak, and he caught a lung disease called pneumonia. Arthur became very ill. Sadly, he didn't live until Valentine's Day—he died on February 6, 1993. He was only 49 years old. Arthur's daughter, Camera, was the same age Arthur was when his own mother died.

Remember how Arthur didn't have many pictures of his mother? Jeanne Ashe didn't want that to happen to Camera. She had taken a lot of photos of Arthur and Camera when Arthur was alive. Later, she published the pictures in a book called *Daddy and Me*.

Arthur Robert Ashe, Jr. was buried in his hometown of Richmond, Virginia. Governor Douglas Wilder gave Arthur a special honor. He had Arthur's

casket displayed in the Governor's Mansion. It was the first time anyone had been honored that way since the Civil War.

Time Line

| 1943 Born | 1960 Moves to St. Louis | 1963 Makes Davis Cup team | 1968 Wins U.S. Open | 1975 Wins at Wimbledon |

Arthur's casket was displayed in the Governor's Mansion. He was buried in Richmond.

1977
Marries

1985 Enters
Tennis Hall of Fame

1992
Addresses U. N.

1993
Dies

The U. S. Open tennis tournament stadium was named after Arthur Ashe.

Time Line

| 1943 Born | 1960 Moves to St. Louis | 1963 Makes Davis Cup team | 1968 Wins U.S. Open | 1975 Wins at Wimbledon |

Court of Champions

Arthur Ashe was an athlete and an activist. We remember him as the first African American man to win the U. S. Open and Wimbledon. And we remember him for his fight to end apartheid and to help those with AIDS.

After his death, Arthur received many honors. In 1996, a bronze statue of him was placed on Monument Avenue in Richmond. In the statue, Arthur is holding a book and a tennis racket. It was designed by Paul DiPasquale of Richmond. In 1997, the stadium where the U. S. Open tennis tournament is played was named Arthur Ashe Stadium. It is located in Queens, New York. Arthur was also awarded honorary degrees from many famous colleges in Virginia and in other states. And in 2009, President Bill Clinton named Arthur to the tennis U. S. Open Court of Champions.

Glossary

activist – A person who speaks out about a problem or takes direct action to help a political cause or belief.

agile – Able to move quickly and easily.

apartheid – A system of government that causes people of different races to be treated differently and keeps them separate.

casket – A type of container in which people are buried.

civil rights movement – A cause that took place during the early 1960s, where people tried to get equal rights for African Americans.

contaminated – To become infected with a germ that causes disease.

match – A sports contest between people or teams.

optimistic – Expecting good things to happen. Thinking positively.

racism – Different or unfair treatment because of someone's race.

scholarship – A gift of money to pay for education.

segregated – The separation of people, usually based on race or religion.

tournament – A series of sports games, or matches, to win a championship.

transfusion – A transfer of blood.

visa – Official permission to enter a country.

Index

Editorial Credits

Designer: Michael Sellner, Corporate Graphics, North Mankato, Minnesota
Consultant/Marketing Design: Alison Hagler, Basset and Becker Advertising, Columbus, Georgia

Image Credits — *All photos © copyright contributor below unless otherwise specified.*

Think With Bagster

Use the information from the book to answer the questions below.

1. Why was it hard for African Americans to become champion tennis players when Arthur was alive?

2. Which events in United States history are similar to apartheid in South Africa? Explain the similarities.

3. Arthur worked hard to succeed at tennis. He also fought against racism. What do these actions say about the kind of person he was?

4. Someone has blamed Bagster for breaking the classroom fish tank, even though he didn't do it. When Arthur was blamed for something he didn't do, he didn't fight back. What would you do?

5. Name some ways Arthur served as a role model for African Americans and for all people.

6. Arhur said, "From what we get, we can make a living; what we give, however, makes a life." What did he mean by this? Name some ways you can give.